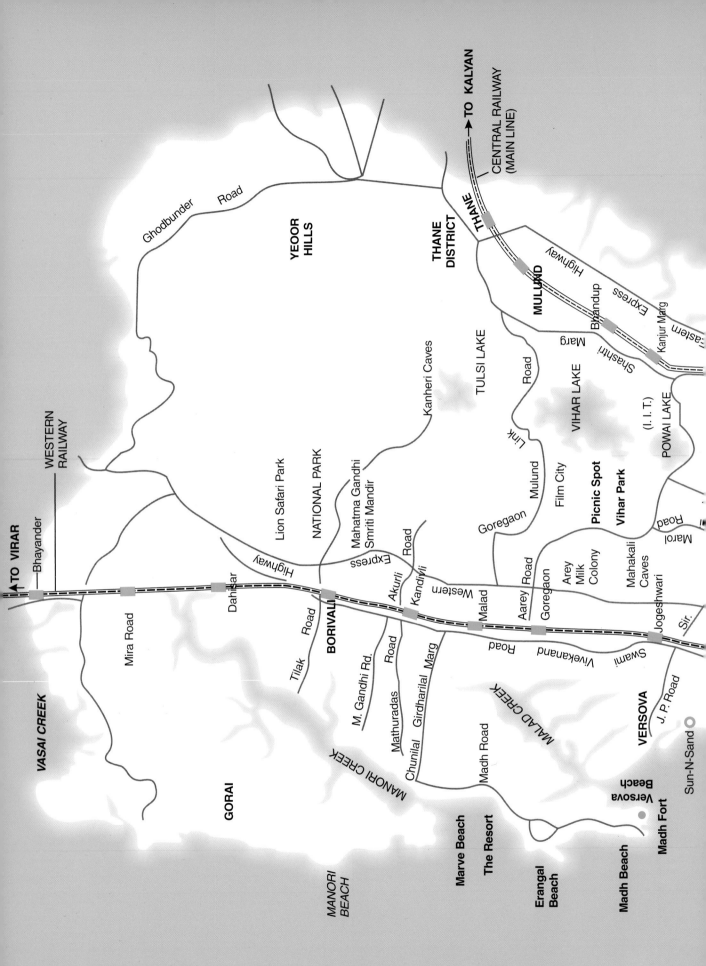

As the golden orb of the sun sets beyond the Arabian sea, the regal silhouette of the Gateway of India stands starkly etched against the dark sky. A monument of magnificent proportions, the Gateway beckons visitors to Bombay, the premier metropolis of India and one of the world's most celebrated cities.

Looking at the sprawling, ten-million-strong city and its highrise skyscrapers, few would believe that Bombay is a very young city. Not so long ago, it was a small cluster of seven islands detached from the subcontinent by turbulent creeks along which lived fishing communities. These original inhabitants of Bombay built a shrine to their goddess – Mumbadevi – on the largest of the islands, later giving the city the name Mumbai. British rulers changed this name to Bombay when India became part of the Empire.

Bombay's history is full of quaint anecdotes. It was ceded by Muslim rulers to the Portuguese in 1549 and sold by them to a botanist for a princely sum of Rs.539! In 1659, when Charles II of England married the Portuguese princess Catherine of Braganza, the islands became part of her dowry and came into the possession of the British.

Over the last three centuries, Bombay has become an integrated land mass with the reclamation of land from the creeks. Today, it is joined to the mainland by bridges, causeways and highways – all busy thoroughfares along which the trade of this great business centre is carried on.

Bombay is one of the great natural ports of the modern world. With its ship-building yards and spacious docks, it is truly the industrial hub of India. Textiles, machinery, electronics, sugar, cotton fibre, food grains and a host of other goods are loaded here in gigantic carriers. In return come petroleum and a variety of raw goods that support the burgeoning industries of the hinterland.

For centuries, Bombay has been a strategic port. The caves and rock-cut shrines that are found around it show that long before its present eminence, the Greeks and Romans traded with the west coast through this island city and brought cave architecture to India. The Dutch, the Portuguese, the Chinese, the British – all came here to buy and sell goods, leaving their cultural imprint on the city's personality. Many are the symbols of this great maritime era which made Bombay a trader's paradise.

Today, Bombay vibrates with activity. People interested in business, education, the arts, travel or leisure, flock to its fantasy world of opportunity and wealth. In Bombay, anyone with talent and tenacity can turn his rags into rich robes almost overnight. This forward-rushing city recognizes only courage and talent and bestows upon the boldest of its citizens, the best of its benefits.

Life in Bombay has its own very special flavour. It is a city that never sleeps. From the time the sun rises over the silver-streaked horizon, till twilight becomes a star-spun cloak over the city, life here enacts an endless drama of events. As the rays of the morning sun touch the city, the serpentine criss-cross of suburban trains – which run day and night – bring millions of men and women to their workplaces. And as dusk settles over the surrounding hills, these same trains and double-decker buses take them to their homes in far-flung suburbs.

All through the working day, Bombay becomes the market place where business worth billions is conducted with international elan; where hard bargains are driven; where fortunes are made or lost by a mere signature on a document.

During these sunlit hours, Bombay also becomes the gourmet's delight. Through a unique relay system, Dabbawalas bring tiffin-carriers filled with home-cooked meals for millions of workers. But those who want to titillate their taste buds can feast upon the country's best variety of Moghlai, Chinese or Western delicacies at breathtakingly beautiful five star hotels and restaurants. Local tongue-ticklers like fish curry and rice, kababs, spicy meat and chicken curries, vegetables cooked in coconut milk and Indian savouries and breads in endless variety are made by small stalls by the roadside called Dhabas. An eating experience here is not complete without the pungent taste of the *pao-bhaji* or *bhel* – both typical of the mix that is Bombay.

The day also means shopping for the connoisseur. Bombay offers him incomparably beautiful jewellery, priceless antiques, shimmering silks and brocades, textiles, furniture and leatherware. A visitor can lose himself in the by-lanes where readymade garments, costume jewellery, paintings, handicrafts, footwear and all kinds of bric-à-brac are sold at attractive prices.

It would seem from the fast-forward lifestyle of Bombay that a visitor never has time to stand and stare. That's not true! Hidden within this frantic activity is a treasure house of sight-seeing marvels. Of all oriental cities, Bombay has successfully preserved superb examples of British neo-Gothic architecture. Victoria Terminus, the High Court, the University and its imposing Rajabai Tower, the Elphinstone College, the Prince of Wales Museum, the Western Railway offices – these are a few of the edifices which show the best features of Gothic architecture with their ornate arches, domes and gargoyles.

An hour's launch ride from the Gateway of India brings the visitor to the island of Elephants where, in different contrast to the neon-lit tempo of the city, time stands still. The cave temples on this island hold 1000-year-old sculptures including the *Trimurti* or the Hindu triad of divinity – the creator, the preserver and the destroyer – depicting the inexorable cycle of life. Here, one waits in the echoing silence of the remote past, admiring works of great value.

Undoubtedly the richest city of India – it pays half the nation's income tax – Bombay celebrates all festivals with noise, pomp and splendour. Perhaps the most colourful of these is Ganesh Chaturthi, when clay idols of Ganesha, the elephant-headed god of auspiciousness and wisdom are worshipped for ten days. On the full moon day in August/September, these idols are immersed in the sea. Thousands gather in the dusk to see this great spectacle of humanity. Diwali, the festival of lights; Holi, the springtime carnival of colour; Janmashtami, the rainy-season celebration of Lord Krishna's birth; Sankranti, the kite flying season; Id, Parsi New Year, Christmas – all these are dear to the fun-loving heart of the Bombayite. Hindus, Muslims, Sikhs, Jains, Christians, Buddhists – all live here in a camaraderie rarely seen elsewhere. No wonder then that cosmopolitan Bombay offers the visitor unique temples, churches and mosques. Of special interest is the Haji Ali mosque set on an offshore island, amidst the lapping waves of the sea.

Though the seasons of the year are not clearly evident in Bombay, the climate is humid and temperate except for April and May. During the summer, the sun shines fiercely, scorching the city's numerous beaches and gardens. The flowering trees of Bombay make the city's streets a festival of colour. By the end of June, the first welcome monsoon showers come, creating a verdant, jewel-green vision. The rains come sometimes in gentle showers, sometimes in torrential downpours, bringing life to a standstill. But Bombay thrives on this season, looking fresh and sparklingly new. It is during the rainbow-hued monsoon that Bombay becomes enchanting and exotic.

One of the greatest attractions of Bombay is its billion-rupee film industry. From far and near, the glamour-struck come here to become stars, to gamble huge amounts on film making, to seek fame and fortune almost overnight. Most famous and glamorous stars like Amitabh Bachchan and Rekha live in mansions or suburban villas, making Bombay the Hollywood of the east.

Dotting the city are green playgrounds, huge stadia, swimming pools and golf courses. Bombay has produced some of India's world famous sports stars. Sunil Gavaskar, Dilip Vengsarkar and many before them began their cricket careers in the by-lanes of the city. Billiards champion Michael Fareira, Badminton ace Prakash Padukone and many others have been nurtured by this sports-loving metropolis.

In a quiet corner of central Bombay lies a nondescript looking playground called the August Kranti Maidan. Here began the famous Quit India movement in 1942. Here too, did Mahatma Gandhi and Jawaharlal Nehru address India's masses to lead them in the struggle for Independence. All over Bombay – at the elegant Flora Fountain, at the Chowpatty Sea Face and in the Fort area – are monuments which remind us of Bombay's stupendous contribution to India's Independence.

Night descends in Bombay on the wings of a glowing, golden dusk and twinkling lights. This is the magical hour when Bombay comes once again to life! Neon lights wink. Street lights turn every road into a jewelled necklace. Night clubs and restaurants are filled with merry-makers who swing to lilting music. Theatres put on plays and spacious halls feature music and dance recitals to please every taste.

All night, the revelry goes on. Music, lights, wine and food create the glittering ambience of a city that is at its best at the midnight hour. Quaint horse-drawn carriages, called Victorias, ply the length of Marine Drive which by night becomes a glittering fairyland of lights.

But too soon, the eastern horizon is ablaze with shards of light. The joggers, the fitness fiends and the brisk walkers get together in the hill-top gardens to share this peaceful hiatus between night and day.

Within an hour, the city is wide awake. Business begins. Shops open. Trains and buses hurtle across the city. The click of typewriters, telephones and machines herald another frenetic day. And the people of Bombay – who are the very soul of this city – begin their journey towards a fruitful, productive day. For them, Bombay is the bridge between a rich past and a promising future.

As the sun rises beyond the Elephanta island and lights up the nuclear reactor in nearby Trombay, Bombay seems poised to launch India into the 21st century . . .

The Nehru Science Centre situated at Worli.

A typical movie house hoarding.

Bustling street in central Bombay.

The Apsara theatre formed in the rather unusual shape of an elephant.

Victoria Terminus popularly known as VT is the Central Railway
Station of Bombay-one of the most famous neo-gothic structures
in the world built in 1888. Victoria Terminus in all its grandeur is
illuminated with colourful lights and decorations in honour of
Republic Day which is commemorated on 26th January each year.
It has now been renamed Chhatrapati Shivaji Terminus

Chhatrapati Shivaji Terminus by day. (formerly Victoria Terminus)

The Taj Mahal Inter-Continental Hotel. This amazing palace of
a hotel was built in 1903 by Jamshedji Tata whose family rank
today amongst the leading industrialists in India. A stay in the
old wing of the Taj is an essential part of a tour of Bombay, indeed
India.

The Gateway of India, built to commemorate the visit of King George V and Queen Mary in 1911

The Vidhan Sabha (Council Hall) looking resplendant on Republic Day.

A local train on the suburban railway system, without which Bombay City would be paralysed.

The Gateway of India.

A common sight in Bombay, the horse-drawn carriage now popularly used for pleasure rides. They are known as Victori

A more leisurely form of transport in this bustling City.

Previous page: The Taj Mahal Inter-Continental Hotel.

Opposite: The Central Tower of Victoria Terminus (Chhatrapati Shivaji Terminus illustrating the true grandeur of this magnificent building.

The Oval Maidan (Park) is to Bombay what Central Park is to New York

Elephanta Island lying in Bombay Harbour contains many temple caves.

The Siddhivinayak Temple.

Sculpture inside the Elephanta Caves.

The statue of Cowasjee Jehangir a noted parsi philanthropist.
(*Above*)

The Maratha Leader Shivaji commemorated for his defiance
against the Moghul Emperors.

Detail of one of the fine lamp-posts at Horniman Circle.

Overleaf: The High Court.

The Ambassador Hotel surmounted by a revolving restaurant.

The Hotel Oberoi Towers. A luxury development in Nariman Point.

The Hotel President situated in Cuffe Parade.

Opposite: The old Council Hall now the Maharashtra Police Headquarters.

Camel cart ride on Juhu Beach.

Juhu Beach at sunset.

Bandra skyline: A suburb of Bombay reflected in the Mahim Bay.

Highrise buildings at Cuffe Parade.

The Shoe. A playhouse for children in Kamala Nehru Park.

White spotted deer in the National Park at Borivli.

Styled hedge in the form of a giraffe in the Hanging Gardens.

Hanging Gardens. A beautiful park situated on the Malabar Hills above South Bombay.

Previous page: The headquarters of the Western Railway, another stunning example of neo-gothic architecture.

Opposite: Chhatrapati Shivaji Terminus (formerly Victoria Terminus)

Traditional buildings at Chowpatti sea face interestingly surmounted by modern neon signs.

Sunset on Malabar Hill close to the Raj Bhawan, the home of the Governor of Bombay.

Malabar Hill. The superior residential locality, viewed from Marine Drive.

Hinduja House. An example of modern construction at the Wo sea face.

Opposite: The headquarters of Bombay Municipal Corporation.

Mahatma Phule market – known by its earlier name of Crawford market. This is the main wholesale vegetable, fruit and poultry market in the City.

An aerial view of the Flora Fountain.

Previous page: Mahatma Gandhi, 'Father of the Nation.'

The Mumbadevi Temple named after the Goddess Mumbai (mother). The name Bombay is derived from Mumbai.

Hamidi Masjid (Mosque)

Dwarkadish Temple – Dedicated to Krishna

The Bullock Cart. This means of transport is still a common sight on the streets of Bombay.

Previous page: Marine Drive in the early evening aptly illustrating the often coined name The Queens Necklace.

A local Pujari.

A Hindu bride.

Typical Parsi family.

Grinding chillies.

Bhori merchant.

Chor Bazaar

Sipping ice – golas

Festive attire

Bridal ornament

श्री महालक्ष्मी मंदिर

Divali. The Festival of Lights. The City of Bombay is ablaze with firecrackers during this Festival.

Mount Mary Church at Bandra on Christmas Eve.

A typical Pujari Holy Priest of the Hindus.

Previous page: Mahalaxmi Temple the abode of the Goddess of Wealth.

A group of Holy Priests taking a dip in the sacred water.

Ganpati Festival – This is Bombay's most popular festival which marks the birthday of Lord Ganesh (God of Intelligence, Luck and Prosperity). For many weeks before the festivities begin clay statues of the Elephant God are being prepared for the many days of worship. Numerous processions take place on the first day and throughout the Festival. Millions turn out on the final day to bid farewell as the effigies of the Lord Ganesh are immersed in the sea from the City's beaches.

Statuette of Ganesha before being dressed up in various glorifying colours.

Crowds on the final day accompanying the effigies of Lord Ganesh and Hanuman (The Monkey God) to the beaches.

The Gokul Ashtami or Matki Festival – this marks the birth of Krishna one of whose pranks was to reach up to a pot of curds which was kept beyond his reach by his mother. This tradition is carried on by forming a human pyramid to reach the pot, suspended high above street level, containing curds mixed with coins.

Sculpture on Juhu Beach of the Gods Ganesh and Shiva.

Fun at Holi on Juhu beach – a Festival of Colours.

This is Ravana the ten headed giant who represents evil. The effigy is loaded with fireworks and ignited. It is quite a memorable sight to watch the fireworks consume the effigy.

Bhavani Durga, Goddess of Strength.

A scene from the Ramayana, a play enacted during the Navratri Festival.

Previous page: The Haji Ali Mosque – situated in the sea. During high tide the mosque is inaccessible from the mainland.

Dwarkadish Temple – dedicated to
Krishna.

Minara Masjid (mosque) in an area
consisting of 95 per cent Muslims.

Hidden amongst the residential
buildings lies the Banganga, a holy pond
in which people take a dip of
purification.

Sacred fire temple of the Parsis.

The snake charmer.

A Parsi family outside their sacred fire temple.

A bridegroom on horseback during Baraat – the family marriage procession.

A handy substitute for the umbrella.

A Marwadi wedding.

Marriage – a symbol of unity.

Opposite: A Koli fisherwoman.

A Haathgadiwala and a Dabawalla – two professions here seen together. The handcart is the cheapest form of transportation in Bombay and the Dabawallas are management wizards in a business so complex it is miraculous it works. Each group of Dabawalls are responsible for collecting the lunch boxes of three to four hundred people from their homes in the morning and transporting them to the many places of work. They also reverse this performance and return the boxes to the same household in the evening. The boxes bear clever identification marks and are very rarely lost or delivered to the wrong person.

The Coconut vendor – the style of cutting the outer shell and serving in Bombay is very unique and quite different from the normal method used elsewhere in India.

The local street dentist.

The Paanwala – selling a combination of betel nuts with other ingredients packed in a leaf which is a munching pleasure.

The Golawalla (above).

Dabawallas.

The ear cleaning business.

The city's traffic policeman.

Fruit for sale in Crawford Market.

Opposite: The Coolie or Railway Porter.

Fishermen on a hand built craft.

Fisherfolk from the Koli Tribe.

A Dhobighat where the laundry men indulge in washing in bulk.

Previous page: Chowpatty Beach

Overleaf: Moods of the Monsoon.

Opposite: A fisherwoman from the Koli tribe drying shrimps.

The Pastiwalla.

Portable shoe polish.

Sugar cane and soaked peanuts vendor.

The Balloonwalla.

Preparing a garland of flowers.

The vegetable vendor.

The Pattiwalla.

The Coolie.

The Channawalla.

Previous page: The Flora Fountain surmounted by the Goddess Flora (Goddess of Flowers).

Opposite: The ever popular vegetable stall.

Evening stalls on Chowpatty Beach.

Bombay's ever changing skyline.

Previous page: Daytime bustle in Kalbadevi District.

Opposite: Sunset over the Haji Ali Mosque.

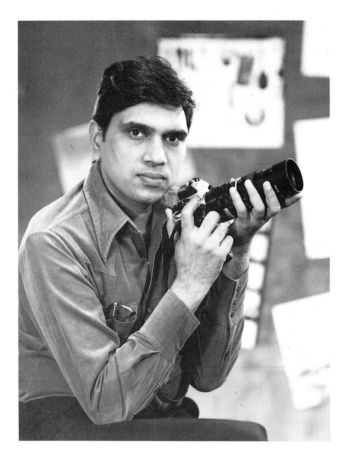

Jagdish Agarwal was born in Haryana, India on July 26th, 1948. He has had a great interest in the Creative Arts and Literature from an early age and during the sixties studied Hindi and English Literature.

In 1964 his uncle presented him with an AGFA box camera and his preoccupation with photography was born and has never since waned.

A photographic course under Professor Pillai at the Indo-American Society marked his first formal training and even at this early stage in his career Jagdish began to win prizes.

By 1974 his work was already being appreciated abroad and in subsequent years he has won many international competitions and awards including the Koishikawa and Accu Awards from Japan, the Photography Contest Award from Pravda (U.S.S.R.) and many other distinguished International and Indian Awards.

Jagdish has contributed to many publications and now runs his own Picture Agency, Dinodia, whilst still managing to run the family textile business.

The following photographers assisted Jagdish Agarwal in compiling this book.

R. A. Acharya	N. M. Kelvalkar	P. Y. Parekh	A. Udeshi
S. D. Bhaumik	R. M. Modi	A. H. Patel	S. N. Sharma
S. G. Gavali	M. C. Morabad	N. G. Sharma	
K. B. Jothady	S. T. Parashar	N. Tank	

All these photographers are contributors to Dinodia Picture Agency.